You can Save the Planet

A Bright Idea:
Conserving Energy

Tristan Boyer Binns

Heinemann Library
Chicago, Illinois

© 2005 Heinemann Library,
a division of Reed Elsevier, Inc.
Chicago, Illinois

Customer Service 888-454-2279
Visit our website at www.heinemannlibrary.com

Designed by Richard Parker and Maverick Design
Illustrations by Q2A and Jeff Edwards
Photo research by Maria Joannou and Virginia Stroud-Lewis
Printed in China by WKT Company Limited

09 08
10 9 8 7 6 5 4 3

Library of Congress Cataloging-in-Publication Data
Binns, Tristan Boyer, 1968-
    A bright idea : conserving energy / Tristan Boyer Binns.
        p. cm. -- (You can save the planet)
Includes bibliographical references and index.
ISBN 1-4034-6844-3 (library binding) -- ISBN 1-4034-6850-8 (pbk.)
ISBN 978-1-4034-6844-4 (HC) -- ISBN 978-1-4034-6850-5 (pbk)
1. Energy conservation--Juvenile literature. I. Title. II. Series.
   TJ163.35.B56 2005
   333.791'6--dc22

                2005000642

Acknowledgments
The author and publishers are grateful to the following for permission to reproduce copyright material:
p. 4 Doug Wilson/Corbis; p. 5 Corbis/; p. 7 David R. Frazier/Science Photo Library; p. 9 Derek Trask/Corbis; pp. 10, 11, 13, 16 Tudor Photography; p. 12 Jim Cummins/Corbis; p. 14 James Leynse/Corbis; p. 15 Rob Lewine/Corbis; p. 17 Hans Strand/Corbis; p. 18 Panos Pictures; p. 19 Robert Harding Picture Library; p. 20 Bernhard Edmaier/Science Photo Library; p. 21 Tony Craddock/Science Photo Library; p. 22 Russell Munson/Corbis; p. 23 Ferdaus Shamim/Corbis; p. 24 John Keating/ Science Photo Library; p. 25 US Dept. of Energy/Science Photo Library; p. 26 Rex Features; p. 27 Stone/Getty Images.

Cover photograph by Rex Features.

Contents

Some words are shown in bold, **like this**. You can find out what they mean by looking in the glossary.

What Is Energy?

Anything that does work uses energy. Work can be many things—your body running, a tomato plant growing, or your television showing you a video. Energy can be turned into different forms and stored.

Most of the energy used on Earth comes from the Sun. Plants turn energy from sunlight into food. Plants then store energy themselves. Heat from the Sun makes the weather. This heat energy is stored in wind, rain, and waves. When we use energy, we take it out of its stored form.

Plant energy

People and other animals use plants for their food. People also use products from plants, such as wood from trees, to burn for **fuel**. Huge numbers of plants and animals died millions of years ago. Their remains were covered by layers of soil and water. Their energy is now stored in oil (petroleum), coal, and natural gas. We call these **fossil fuels**.

When wood is burned, its energy is released as heat and light.

4

What Does Energy Do For Us?

People have always used energy to help make their lives easier. Long ago, simple machines such as levers used people's muscles for power. As machines became more complex they needed more power than people could give. Animals pulled plows to help grow food. Mills that used wind or water for power ground wheat into flour.

Today we rely on very complex machines such as refrigerators and cars. Most modern machines are powered by electricity or engines that run on oil. Most of the power we use comes from fossil fuels. It is hard to imagine life without our machines and the energy that powers them.

Some machines use energy to keep us healthy. This MRI machine can produce a picture of the inside of your body, but it needs electricity to run.

Taking Action

If we keep using so much energy, we are storing up problems for people in the future. You might think that the problem of saving, or conserving, energy is too big for you to do anything about. But if each of us makes a small effort, together we can make a big difference. Look for Taking Action boxes like this one throughout this book. They will give you ideas for things you can do to conserve energy.

Getting energy home

Most of the energy we use at home and in school comes to us as electricity. It is made in an electricity factory called a **power plant**.

We also use other kinds of energy in our daily lives. Energy is used to make the things we buy, from clothes to boxes of cereal. The trucks that transport these things to stores use energy. We use all kinds of **fuels** directly. Gasoline engines drive our cars, gas boilers heat our homes and water, and gas or electric stoves cook our food.

Science Behind It: Making Electricity

Inside a power plant, fuel is used to drive a **turbine**. It usually heats water to make steam, which turns the turbine. The turbine looks like a pinwheel or propeller. As it spins, it makes an electricity **generator** work. The generator sends the electricity along wires to us.

furnace

fuel

steam

turbine

generator

power lines

water

Why Do We Need to Conserve Energy?

You might think there is no need to conserve energy. Whenever you flip a switch, there is enough electricity to turn on the lights. But using too much energy has effects that are harder to see.

First, we are running out of **fossil fuels**. Fossil fuels are still forming in Earth, but the process takes millions of years. Before the end of your life, we may run out of oil and gas. If we can use fewer fossil fuels now, the supply we have now will last longer.

Also, when we burn fossil fuels for energy they give off gases. Some of these gases **pollute** our air and water. This can make the air unsafe to breathe and the water unsafe to drink. One of the main gases produced is **carbon dioxide**. Carbon dioxide is not bad by itself. Plants need it to make their food. The problem is that we are making too much of it.

In cities where a great deal of fossil fuels are burned, the air looks hazy because of pollution.

Climate change happens naturally over long periods of time. We may be making it happen faster by adding gases such as carbon dioxide, which many scientists believe is causing the planet to heat up. If Earth's **climate** changes, it could cause many problems for people and other living things.

Science Behind It: The Greenhouse Effect

Carbon dioxide in the air can form a invisible shield, like a pane of glass in a greenhouse. The Sun's heat gets in through the shield, but then it gets trapped. The extra heat is making our planet warm up. This is called the greenhouse effect.

3. Waste gases in the air can trap the heat

1. The Sun's heat warms the land and the sea

2. The warm land and sea give off heat

Making Changes

We can help prevent these problems. One way is to find other sources of energy. Some types, such as wind and solar power, are **renewable**. They are made by the Sun and cannot be used up. Another way is to use energy more **efficiently** so we waste less.

How Is Energy Wasted?

At home and at school, energy is used and wasted in similar ways. Scientists think that we waste about half of the heating energy we use.

Energy keeping us warm

At home, we use the most energy for heating. All of these waste energy:

- badly **insulated** walls
- cracks in floorboards and around doors and windows
- drafty windows
- lofts without insulation
- uninsulated hot-water pipes and tanks
- water heated hotter than we need
- room heat turned up high when an extra sweater would do
- windows or doors left open when the heating or air conditioning is on
- curtains left open on a cold night

Transportation wastes

Taking the car more than you need to wastes more energy than biking, walking, or taking the bus or train. Could you combine errands and make one trip instead of many? Could you share a ride?

Traveling with only one person in a car wastes a lot of energy. Sharing rides or going by **public transportation** saves energy, and puts less **carbon dioxide** into the air.

Wasting electricity

Whenever you waste electricity, you waste energy. If you do any of these things, you will waste electricity:

- leaving lights on when you leave a room
- leaving machines on or in sleep mode. Many photocopiers, computers, and televisions are left on overnight
- leaving the refrigerator door open

Machines such as cars, boilers, and lawnmowers work best when they are properly maintained. For example, changing dirty filters and keeping fluids topped up will help a car use energy more **efficiently**.

Science Behind It: Losing Power

Every way of making power costs energy. For example, batteries take 50 times as much energy to make as they can give out. When coal is burned in a **power plant** only some of its energy is made into electricity. Most of the rest is lost as heat. More energy is lost as the electricity travels along wires to buildings.

These machines can use almost as much energy in sleep mode as they do when turned on completely.

How Can We Conserve Energy?

Every day, you make hundreds of choices. Some will save energy and some will use it. You have the power to make choices that will help change the Earth for the better.

Reduce, reuse, recycle

Energy is used every time something new is made. Here is a great way to start conserving energy: reduce what you use, reuse what you can, and **recycle** as much of your waste as possible. For example, reduce the number of plastic bags you use by bringing old ones with you when you shop. When they cannot be used anymore, most supermarkets will take them back to recycle.

Taking Action: Using Less

Here are some other ways to reduce and reuse around your home:
- reuse envelopes
- draw or write on both sides of paper
- send e-cards instead of paper ones
- use libraries and rental stores instead of buying new books, videos, or DVDs
- wash out and reuse sandwich bags and water bottles
- use cloths and sponges instead of paper towels
- give old clothes and appliances to resale shops instead of throwing them out

Recycled plastic can be used to make many things, such as these fleece jackets and garbage bags.

Using less energy

Around the house and at school, you can make energy-saving choices. Simply turning off things when you finish using them will help a lot. When a television or computer is in sleep mode it still uses energy, so switch it off completely. Turn lights off when you leave a room. Dry your clothes and wet hair in the open air when you can. Only run the dishwasher or washing machine when they are full.

It takes energy to heat water. It also takes energy to make water clean and get it to our houses to use. You can choose to save water and save energy, too. Take a shower instead of a bath—this will save both water and energy! Do not leave the tap running while you wash the dishes or brush your teeth.

Taking Action: Free Time

One more way to conserve energy is to think about what you do for fun. Shopping and playing computer games use electricity. What do you do that does not use electricity? Playing basketball, chatting with your friends, or reading—what else? These all use a type of **renewable** energy—yours!

Playing ball games uses a lot of energy, but you do not have to burn any **fossil fuels** to do it!

Making Choices

Some of the best ways to conserve energy are to choose more **efficient** ways to do things. You need light bulbs to light the rooms in your house. Replacing regular light bulbs with special low-energy ones saves a huge amount of energy.

Low-energy light bulbs can use nearly 70 percent less energy than regular bulbs. Low-energy light bulbs also last up to ten times longer.

Some family choices can make big savings. When your family needs new appliances, look at the energy labels to choose the most efficient ones. When your parents are choosing a car, encourage them to get one that will use the least amount of **fuel**.

Using the Internet or catalogs to shop saves energy. Items ordered online or from a catalog are stored in big warehouses that cost less to run than smaller stores and shops. A delivery truck delivers items to many households, which takes less energy than would be used if each family drove to and from a store to buy the items.

Saving energy on food

You can choose food grown or made near your home by shopping at farmers' markets. Food grown near your community does not have to travel far, so it takes less energy to produce. The packaging your food comes in takes energy, too. Think about all the food boxes and drink bottles you throw away. Could you save energy and waste by reusing bags and bottles to make home-packaged snacks and drinks?

All this waste took energy to produce. It took energy to bring it to this landfill site too.

The way to school

In developed countries such as the United States and Great Britain, driving children to school uses a huge amount of energy. Walking or biking may be a great way to save energy and help keep you fit. School buses use a lot of gasoline, which is made from oil (petroleum). They can be changed to run on cleaner fuel and use less energy.

Taking Action: Transport Savings

You can help save energy getting to school. You could start a group working with other students, parents, and teachers. Take **surveys** of how people get to school. Look into other ways you could get to school using less fuel.

Case Study: Saving Energy at School

Students can look at how their school uses energy and find ways to conserve it. Sulzberger Middle School in Philadelphia, Pennsylvania, joined the Green Schools program. It won an Earth Apple award for how well it saved energy. Students and teachers worked together. They made posters saying "Save Energy." They made a video about saving energy. They also formed an Energy Patrol. The Energy Patrol looked for classrooms that wasted energy by leaving windows open, lights on, and blinds up. They fined energy wasters 10 cents.

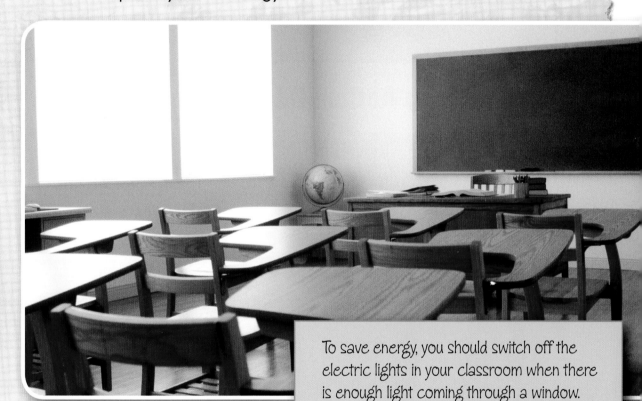

To save energy, you should switch off the electric lights in your classroom when there is enough light coming through a window.

Success!

After one school year, no one was fined anymore. Sulzberger Middle School saved 194,230 kilowatt hours of electricity. This was almost half of what they had used the year before! Savings this high mean good things for Earth. Such savings also mean the school has more money to spend on books and other materials.

CASE STUDY

What Is the Problem with Fossil Fuels?

There are three kinds of **fossil fuels**: coal, oil (petroleum), and natural gas. Of these, we have the most coal left. But coal is not used as much as it once was, since it is more **polluting** and less **efficient** to burn. We have about 70 years' worth of natural gas left. This is cleaner to burn and can be burned in homes to power their heating systems. This makes it more efficient.

We only have about 40 years' worth of oil left, because we use it so quickly. Oil is made into many things including gasoline and jet **fuel**.

Taking Action: Oil in the Home

Make a list. How many of these things are in your life? These are all made from oil:
- plastic bags
- tires
- plastic toys
- food wrappers
- nylon and polyester clothes

What other materials could you use now to replace plastics? How could you use less in the first place?

Oil can be made into chemicals that are used to make plastic items.

What Other Kinds of Fuel Are There?

Fossil fuels power most of the world. But other fuels are used more and more. Different places can use different kinds of fuel.

In some places, the hot liquid rock inside Earth is fairly close to the surface. The hot rock heats water in the ground above it. The water comes out as hot springs or steam. It can be turned into **renewable geothermal** energy. Geothermal energy is not perfect. Some pollution comes out of the ground with the steam. Some **carbon dioxide** is given off. But the amounts are very low compared to burning fossil fuels.

Science Behind It: Geothermal Power

In a **power plant**, fuel is usually burned to make steam that then turns a **turbine**. A geothermal power plant simply skips the burning stage. The steam comes directly from the ground and then turns the turbines. Electricity is made and sent along wires. Geothermal power can also make hot water and steam heat to be sent straight to homes.

In Iceland, geothermal energy is used for most of the electricty and heating. These people are swimming in the hot water near the power station!

What is bioenergy?

Everything that comes from plants and animals is called **biomass**. Biomass can be used to make **bioenergy**. Bioenergy makes no more carbon dioxide than the biomass would give off if it **decayed** naturally. Because biomass comes from growing things, it is renewable.

The most popular kind of biomass is wood. Many people burn wood in their homes for cooking and heating. Huge **power plants** also burn wood and other plants to make electricity. Biomass can also be made into liquid **biofuels**. Some biofuel is made from the vegetable oil left over from making french fries! Biofuel can also be made from plants such as sugar cane. After the sugar is removed, the waste cane can be made into biofuel. Biofuels can be added to or used instead of gasoline.

This is a biogas generator being used to make power for a home in Nepal.

When biomass is heated in a closed space, it gives off a gas. This gas can be used for energy. Farming families in poor countries can use small systems to change their animal manure into this **biogas** to cook and heat with. A bigger system can collect the biogas given off by garbage in a landfill site. The biogas is burned in power plants to make electricity.

18

Nuclear power

A nuclear power plant has a **reactor** where **uranium** fuel is used to heat water. The hot water makes steam, just as it does in fossil-fuel power stations. The steam turns a turbine to make electricity.

Nuclear power is not renewable, because the uranium has to be dug from the ground. We will eventually run out of uranium. Nuclear power makes no carbon dioxide, so it does not add to **climate change**. But it does make very dangerous waste. Some gets into the air and water near power plants. It can make people and animals very ill. Uranium waste can stay dangerous for more than 10,000 years. How to store nuclear waste safely is an important issue that scientists are always working on.

Science Behind It: Splitting Atoms

A nuclear reactor makes heat by splitting **atoms** of uranium into even smaller parts. When they split, they give off energy. This reaction is controlled very carefully. If not done correctly, it can be very dangerous and can result in many people being injured or killed.

This is a nuclear power station by the sea.

Water power

Water can be used to make electricity. Water power is renewable. **Hydroelectric** power plants use dams across rivers to trap water. Tidal power plants trap water behind gates in rivers as the tide comes in. When power is needed, the trapped water is let out. The rushing water turns the turbines. The turbines make generators run that make electricity.

Waves can also make power. As they rise and fall, they move air inside a tube. The moving air turns a turbine. But waves have so much power they break the machines easily.

Many people think that the costs from huge dam projects are higher than the benefits of clean electricity.

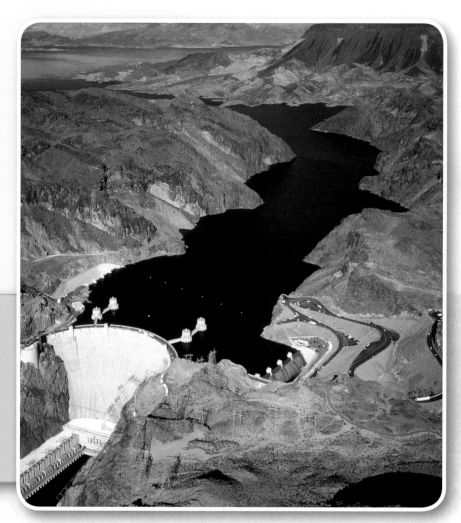

When dams and tidal gates are built, they flood land. Big projects mean whole towns and farms are lost. The places where plants and animals live are gone forever. Small projects can still make enough power for a town without hurting the land around it.

Solar power

In places where it is very sunny, solar energy can be used. The Sun's energy is renewable. It can be used in a number of ways. It can be focused by mirrors onto one spot. Solar stoves use the focused energy to cook a family's meal. Solar power plants use the energy to make steam. The steam spins the turbines and makes electricity.

This is a huge sunlight reflector in France.

In many homes, solar energy heats water. Pipes are built into panels on the roof. Cold water enters the pipes, is heated by the Sun, and then flows into the hot-water tank.

Science Behind It: Solar Panels

Solar panels contain cells that are made from a material called **silicon**. The panels take sunlight and turn it directly into electricity. They are expensive to make. It takes a lot of them to make enough power for the needs of a whole house. But they can be used anywhere, and they do not break down. Thousands of panels linked together can run solar power plants.

Hi-tech windmills

In places where it is windy a lot of the time, windmills can be used to collect energy. Wind energy is renewable. Most of today's windmills have blades that look like airplane propellers. They spin and turn gears inside the windmill. The gears turn an electricity **generator**. One windmill can power a single home. Grouped together in a wind farm they can make a huge amount of power.

This wind farm uses a lot of land but makes a lot of electricity.

Sight and sound

Windmills are huge. The blades are high up, where the wind is strongest, so they are hard to hide. Many people think wind farms are ugly. Windmills make no air **pollution**, but they do make noise pollution. Sometimes wind farms can be built in shallow water off a coastline. They cost more to build there, but they make more power and are farther away from where people live.

Batteries and fuel cells

The problem with solar and wind energy is that they depend on weather or **climate** conditions, so they cannot be used everywhere. Batteries and **fuel cells** store power so they can be used no matter what the weather.

Batteries are made from chemicals that give off power when they react with each other. Small batteries run small things such as toys, but big ones can power a house. Fuel cells are much more **efficient** than batteries at making power. They can run spacecraft and cars. Most are recharged with hydrogen.

Science Behind It: How a Fuel Cell Works

Water is made up of hydrogen and oxygen. A fuel cell is charged with hydrogen. When power is needed, it pulls oxygen from the air. The oxygen mixes with the hydrogen to make water. When the water is made, energy is given off for the fuel cell to use as electricity. The water and power are the only things the fuel cell makes. It does not make any pollution.

This is a car with a fuel cell engine, which makes no pollution.

Case Study: Eco Schools

Schools in Europe can join the Eco Schools program. The program has many ideas for how to make schools more Earth-friendly. One focus is on energy. Wilnecote Junior School is an Eco School in England that runs on electricity. The school wanted to save money and use less electricity.

This building has lots of solar panels to make electricity. Could you use a solar panel at home or school?

Solar walkway

Students and teachers came up with a plan to build a walkway with a solar panel on the top. The solar panel makes enough power to light classrooms and run computers. To tell people about their success, the school has a display by the office. The display says how much power is being made at any time, and how much has been made since the panel was put in. Wilnecote still has to buy some electricity but much less than before.

Paying for the change

Wilnecote did not have to pay for the whole cost of the project by itself. The government and some businesses paid half of the money. In some countries, governments offer **grants** of money like this to schools and people who want to be more energy-**efficient**.

Biomass central heating

In Slovenia, one Eco School has made a big change. Students and teachers at the Sv. Trojica primary school looked at how their school used energy. They decided to change the way the central heating system was powered. After looking at their **renewable** energy choices, they chose to use a **biomass** boiler. Their boiler burns wood to heat the school.

Opening Ceremony

When the new boiler was ready to run, Sv. Trojica had an opening ceremony. They invited students and important people from their town. The president of the Slovenian biomass group helped out. Sv. Trojica is proud to be the only school in Slovenia using wood biomass for its heating system.

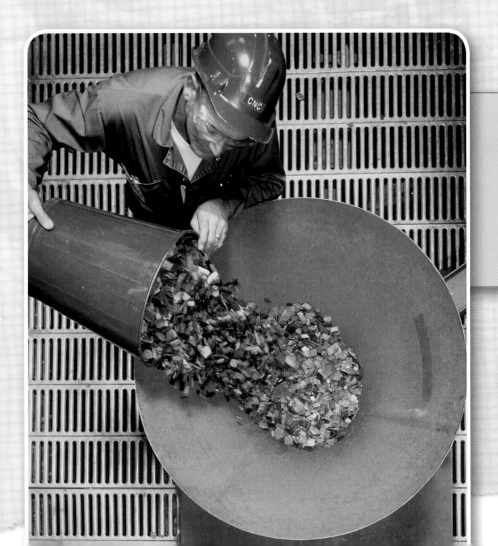

This man is putting wood chips into a machine to make the **fuel** for a biomass boiler.

What Will Happen Next?

As we run out of **fossil fuels** and create more **pollution**, we will have to use more and more **renewable** energy. Even though we already have some good sources of renewable energy, new sources are being researched every day.

Cool water makes cool air

Some experts look at what we need instead of focusing on how to get it. In Ithaca, New York, there is a big lake full of cool water. In the heat of the summer, the cool water could be pumped to shore. It could make cool air for air conditioning. The water would cool hot air in a heat exchanger. The warmed water would run back into the lake but would not be hot enough to harm wildlife. This is also being tried in other cities by big lakes in Sweden, Canada, and the United States.

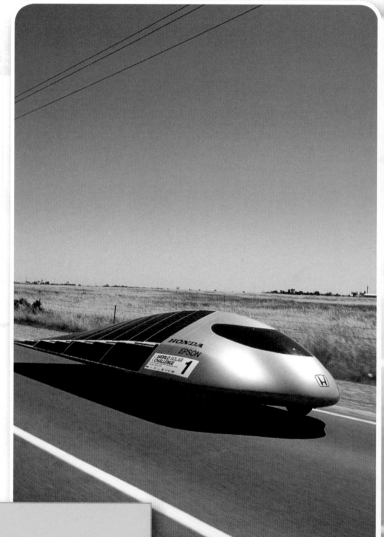

The American Solar Challenge shows how well renewable energy can work. This 2,300-mile (3,700-kilometer) car race is only open to cars that run on solar power.

Fuel cells

New kinds of **fuel cells** look very promising. One type is made with natural gas. It does not actually burn the gas. Instead, it uses a chemical reaction to make the power. This fuel cell is very quiet, gives off little pollution, and seems very **efficient**. Even though it still uses a fossil fuel, it uses the **fuel** in a better way.

There is a kind of algae that gives off hydrogen. If enough hydrogen could be collected from the algae, it could be used to power hydrogen fuel cells. Other types of plants may help make more **bioenergy**. A special kind of seaweed grows up to three feet (one meter) a day. If it was farmed and used to make **biogas**, it could produce a lot of power.

Taking Action: Energy Club

Using what you have learned so far, think about how you could use renewable energy in your home or school. How can you save energy as well? Start an energy club and research what would work for you and your friends.

Some newer kitchen appliances contain computers that control how they work. This means they work more efficiently and use less energy.

27

fact file

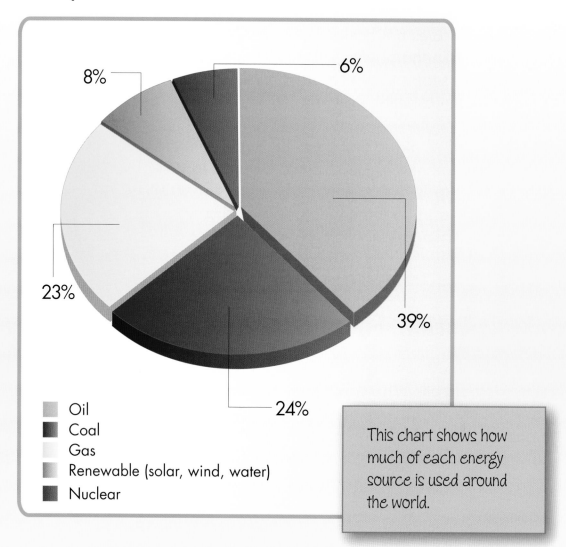

6%

8%

23%

39%

24%

Oil
Coal
Gas
Renewable (solar, wind, water)
Nuclear

This chart shows how much of each energy source is used around the world.

- In Britain, private cars are responsible for 80 percent of the energy used for transportation.
- In rural China, two-thirds of homes use **biogas**.
- In the United States, almost 4 percent of all energy used is **bioenergy**.
- In Britain, almost 3 percent of energy comes from **renewable** sources.

Further Reading

Graham, Ian. *Earth's Precious Resources: Fossil Fuels*. Chicago: Heinemann Library, 2004.

Hawkes, Nigel. *New Energy Sources*. Danbury, Conn.: Franklin Watts, 2000.

Morgan, Sally. *Alternative Energy Sources*. Chicago: Heinemann Library, 2002.

Glossary

atom smallest part of a chemical, such as an atom of oxygen

bioenergy energy made from biomass

biofuel fuel made from biomass, such as vegetable oil

biogas gas made from biomass, such as methane gas

biomass everything that comes from plants and animals, including manure

carbon dioxide gas made from carbon and oxygen that adds to climate change. It is also used by plants to make their food.

climate what the temperature, wind, humidity, rainfall, and other weather is like in an area

climate change as we add to the layer of gases that surround Earth, different climates around the world may get warmer or colder, wetter or dryer. No one is sure how much change will happen.

decay what happens after things die when they break down and rot

efficient using a resource, such as energy or water, so that as little as possible is wasted

fossil fuel fuel that is formed from the remains of plants and animals that died millions of years ago. Fossil fuels include coal, gas, and oil (petroleum).

fuel something that can be burned to create heat or power

fuel cell machine that makes power from hydrogen

generator machine that makes energy

geothermal describes energy that comes from the heat deep within Earth

grant money given to help buy or change something, such as changing the kind of fuel an engine uses to a less polluting one

hydroelectric electricity made from water as it flows over turbines

insulate keep heat, sound, or electricity from escaping and being wasted

pollution something that makes air, water, or other parts of Earth's environment dirty

power plant place where electricity is made

public transportation buses, trains, trams, and any kind of transportation that can be used by many people

reactor place in a nuclear power plant where uranium is used to make heat and then power

recycle collect things made from a material that can be broken down and remade into new things, such as newspapers, plastic, or glass bottles

renewable something that does not run out when we use it, such as solar energy

silicon material that helps change sunlight into electricity in solar panels

survey list of questions and answers that helps you find out people's opinions and ideas

turbine machine driven by water or steam that turns or spins

uranium material that comes from Earth that can be used to make nuclear power

Index